THE TRUE KING

Scripture is taken from The Holy Bible, English Standard Version, ESV®. Copyright © 2001 by Crossway Bibles, a publishing ministry of Good News Publishers.

Published by 10Publishing, a division of 10ofThose Limited.

ISBN: 978-1-914966-19-4

10Publishing, a division of 10ofthose.com
Unit C, Tomlinson Road, Leyland, Lancashire, PR25 2DY England
Email: info@10ofthose.com
Website: www.10ofthose.com

Written by Nancy Guthrie
Illustrated by Jenny Brake
Designed by Diane Warnes

THE TRUE KING

WRITTEN BY NANCY GUTHRIE
ILLUSTRATED BY JENNY BRAKE

10 Publishing
a division of 10 ofthose.com

There are lots of books that tell stories about kings and kingdoms, princes and princesses.

But there's just one problem with all of these stories: they aren't true. They are nice stories, but they are not true stories.

There is one book, however, that tells a grand story about a king and a kingdom, that is the truest story ever told. This is the story of the True King who rules over his people in perfect goodness in a kingdom that will last forever.

This is the story of the Bible. This story doesn't begin with "once upon a time." Instead, it begins at the very beginning of time.

> "In the beginning, God created the heavens and the earth"
>
> Genesis 1:1

The Bible begins by telling us that God is the Great King over his kingdom. His kingdom is the heavens and earth that he created from nothing. At the heart of his kingdom was once a beautiful garden called Eden where Adam and Eve lived, enjoying the goodness of the Great King.

Adam and Eve were told to have many children and extend the edges of Eden, so that all of the wilderness outside Eden would become a fruitful garden filled with glad subjects of the Great King.

The Great King planted all kinds of trees in Eden from which Adam and Eve could eat. But there was one tree from which they could not eat. It was called the tree of the knowledge of good and evil. If they ate fruit from this forbidden tree, they would die.

Everything about life in the garden kingdom was good... perfectly good... until...

A rival kingdom invaded Eden. A lying serpent told Eve that what the Great King said about the forbidden tree wasn't true. He said Adam and Eve could be king and queen in their own kingdom. He said the fruit of the forbidden tree was good and would make them wise.

But it was a lie. And when Adam and Eve rebelled against the Great King and ate from the forbidden tree, everything changed. Adam and Eve went from enjoying the Great King to hiding from him.

The Great King cursed the serpent and the ground, and the impact of that curse was felt throughout the kingdom. The Great King also told Adam and Eve that things that once made them happy would became hard. Instead of enjoying life forever in the garden, they would one day die and be buried in the dust of the earth.

The Great King also made a promise of grace. He promised that one day a baby would be born who would be the True King. A son of the serpent would bring him great harm, but the True King would overcome, crush the serpent's head, and put an end to the serpent's evil.

Because they disobeyed God, Adam and Eve were forced out of the kingdom of Eden into the wilderness of the world. But the Great King was not content for his people to live far away from him and his blessing. He began working out his plan to bring his people back into his kingdom.

He did this by declaring war on the power of sin and death. Ever since then, two opposing forces have been at war in the world: the kingdom of the Great King and the kingdom of the evil serpent.

God began working out his plan to bring his people back to himself by making incredible, undeserved promises to a man named Abraham.

God promised Abraham that he would be the father of a family that would grow to become a great nation, a royal people. God promised that he would give his people the land of Canaan where they would live under his loving rule and enjoy his blessing.

The family grew. When there was a famine, they went to Egypt to find food. There the battle between the kingdom of the Great King and the kingdom of the evil serpent continued to rage. Pharaoh, a son of the serpent, sought to kill all of Abraham's family.

But God sent Moses to bring God's people out of Egypt so they could serve the Great King instead of the cruel Pharaoh. He gave them his law so they would know how to live in his land and be his holy people.

Then he brought them into his land in Canaan. If they stayed true to the Great King, they would live there enjoying his blessing forever.

God, the Great King, promised to give his people a human king, a king who would protect them in power and rule over them in goodness.

Many years later, a boy named David from a place called Bethlehem tended his father's sheep. One day, when he was out in a field, he was called home. Samuel, the Great King's servant, had come to make it known that David would be king over Israel.

David went to see his brothers on the battlefield. A Philistine named Goliath, who was covered in armor that looked like the skin of a snake, was threatening the people of God with slavery to the Philistines. Young David went out alone to do battle with Goliath. With one stone flung from his slingshot, David crushed Goliath's head.

Just as God made Abraham an incredible promise, God also made David an incredible promise. God promised David that one of his sons would become king after him, and that this son's kingdom would last forever.

Solomon became king after David, and everyone wondered if Solomon was the son God had promised whose kingdom would last forever. Solomon's kingdom was very great! He built the temple in Jerusalem for the Great King to live in among his people. Solomon had great riches and great wisdom, and under him God's people enjoyed a life of peace.

When Solomon died, one of his sons became the next king. In fact, for four hundred years David's sons and grandsons, and their sons and grandsons, became king. And while some of these kings did some good things, many did great evil.

Instead of loving and enjoying the goodness of the Great King alone, they looked for happiness and safety in other kingdoms. None of these kings turned out to be the True King that God had promised.

Sadly, the day came when God's people became so evil that they were forced to leave God's land. They were taken away to live in a faraway kingdom called Babylon.

After seventy years in Babylon, some of God's people made their way back to the land that the Great King had given to them. There they began to wait.

They waited for one of David's sons to establish a kingdom that would last forever. They waited a very long time. Some of God's people grew tired of waiting and gave up looking for the coming of the True King.

But then an angel appeared to a young girl named Mary. The angel told Mary that she was going to have a son and that her son would be a king like David. The angel said that his kingdom would last forever.

And sure enough, in David's royal city, the True King was born into this world. The Son of the Great King left the glory of his Father's heavenly kingdom to be born on the earth as a baby. They named him Jesus. He would save his people from their sins.

But Jesus didn't really seem like a king. Kings are born in palaces, but Jesus was born in a cattle stall. Kings expect to be served, but Jesus came to serve. Kings are surrounded by noblemen, but Jesus was surrounded by fishermen. Kings wear crowns of gold, but Jesus was given a crowns of thorns.

Jesus is not a king like other kings of this world. And his kingdom is not like other kingdoms of this world.

Jesus taught people to pray to the Great King, "May your kingdom come, and your will be done on earth as it is in heaven." In heaven, everything is exactly as it should be. Nothing is spoiled by sin. All who live in the kingdom of heaven obey the Great King and enjoy his goodness.

Jesus taught his people to pray for the kingdom of heaven to come to earth. And one day it will.

During his time on earth, Jesus, the True King, helped his people see what life will be like when God's heavenly kingdom comes to earth.

He healed people with diseases, showing that sickness will have no place in his kingdom when it comes.

He commanded demons to leave, because nothing evil will have a place in his coming kingdom.

He made a storm stop, showing that all nature obeys his command in his kingdom.

He fed crowds of people, giving them a taste of the goodness in his kingdom.

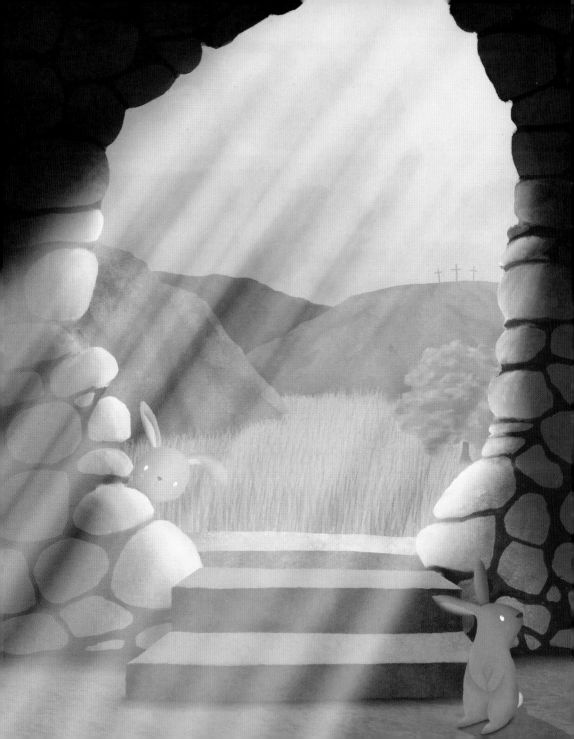

Jesus welcomed all people to come into his kingdom by putting their trust in him. And the rival kingdom didn't like that. So the war continued between the kingdom of the Great King and the kingdom of the ancient serpent. The serpent did his best to destroy Jesus. He put into the hearts of some people the desire to kill Jesus.

When the True King was put to death on a cross, his enemies thought they were putting an end to his kingdom. They didn't know that in his death God was pouring out the punishment guilty people deserve on his innocent son, so that his people could live in his presence forever.

The body of Jesus was put in a grave. But three days later, he came back to life. By overcoming death, Jesus, the True King, crushed the head of the ancient serpent.

Jesus spent forty days with his people, teaching them more about his kingdom. And then he went up into the heavens. The Great King poured out his Spirit on his people, giving them power to take the good news of his kingdom to people all over the earth.

Right now the True King is seated at the right hand of the Great King in heaven. The kingdom of God is spreading across the world as the good news of the True King goes out and is embraced by all who turn away from sin and believe in Jesus.

God's kingdom comes now as people bow to Jesus as their True King.

The people of the kingdom are those who long for the True King to come to this earth again. And one day he will!

They long for the True King to punish evil and reward what is good. And one day he will!

They long for the grace and truth of the True King to spread to every corner the world. And one day it will!

One day his kingdom will come. His will will be done on this earth in same way it is done now in heaven. Heaven will come to earth when Jesus, the True King of heaven, comes again to earth. On that day earth will become heaven.

When Jesus, the True King, comes again, he will destroy the ancient serpent so that he will never hurt the people of the kingdom again.

When Jesus, the True King, comes again, all creation will be made new. It will be like a garden even better than Eden. All of the people who have been saved by the King will live together in God's land.

"at the name of Jesus every knee should bow, in heaven and on earth and under the earth, and every tongue will confess that Jesus Christ is Lord, to the glory of God the Father"

Philippians 2:10-11

His land will extend to every corner of the earth. Every person whose name is written in God's Book of Life will live there under the rule of the King of kings.

On that day when the True King comes again, God's people will hear the glad news they have longed to hear ever since Adam and Eve had to leave the Great King's garden,

ever since God called Abraham to be the father of a royal people

ever since Moses brought them out of Egypt to be a holy nation

ever since God promised David a throne that would last forever

ever since Jesus ascended to his throne in heaven.

All will hear:

> "The kingdom of the world has become the kingdom of our Lord and of his Christ, and he shall reign forever and ever"
>
> Revelation 11:15

There is only one kingdom that proves true,

one kingdom that will last forever,

one kingdom with a king who is able to reign over this world and in our hearts forever.

We long for our True King to come! So we pray to the Great King, "Our Father in heaven, may your name be honored, may your kingdom come."

ABOUT THE AUTHOR

Nancy Guthrie teaches the Bible at her home church, Cornerstone Presbyterian Church in Franklin, Tennessee, as well as at conferences around the country and internationally. She is the host of the Help Me Teach the Bible podcast from The Gospel Coalition and the author of numerous books, including One Year of Dinner Table Devotions and What Every Child Should Know About Prayer.

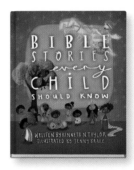

 **Publishing**

10Publishing is committed to publishing
quality Christian resources that are biblical,
accessible and point people to Jesus.

www.10ofthose.com is our online retail partner
selling thousands of quality books at discounted prices.

For information contact: info@10ofthose.com
or check out our website: www.10ofthose.com